Symphony Of

SOULS

"Poetry is Our Music"

THE POETRY ALLIANCE

SYMPHONY OF SOULS

SYMPHONY OF SOULS

Copyright © 2014 THE POETRY ALLIANCE

Printed in the United States of America

ISBN-13: 978-0692372135
ISBN-10: 069237213X

Printed by Createspace 2014
Published by BlaqRayn Publishing Plus 2014

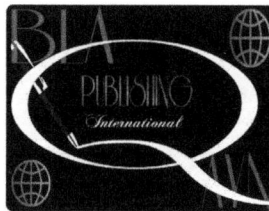

Cover Design by: Jp Parsons

Author Participation

❧

Billy Charles Root
Romeo Della Valle
Olfa Drid
Eden Hundsdoerfer
Debbie Harman
Dennis John Ferado
David Hall
Margaret Gudkov
Debbie Rice
Joe Wilson
Richard J. Panizza
Jahanshah Rashidian
Fatima Coutinho
Antonio Duarte
Rose Mary McKenzie
Elluisa Granath - Vargas Conroy
Thaddeus Hutyra
Ken Blick

❧

SYMPHONY OF SOULS

Introduction

Symphony of Souls

This work brings together creative writers of different nationalities, differing cultures, and different ages and languages. We all have one thing in common, however; we are all passionate about the written word in this creative format. You will see several different styles and genres, and we believe that this is what makes **The Poetry Alliance** work. We accept our differences as we all search for the hint that will send each of us in a new creative direction. This collection of poems is the second book published by **The Poetry Alliance**. The first book '*Land of Souls: Where the Light of Shadows Fall*' is available via Amazon.

The Poetry Alliance is an eclectic group of creative writers who hail from many different countries. Within this volume there are poets from Belgium, Brazil, Germany, the United States of America, the United Kingdom, and Tunisia. Each has contributed five poems towards this collection and on a variety of subjects. The creator of this group, **Ken Blick** is one of the contributors to this collection as is **Thaddeus Hutyra** who has been a moving force in gathering the work together for publication.

We hope you enjoy reading this book.

Joe Wilson

Symphony of

SOULS

The Poetry Alliance

SYMPHONY OF SOULS

ষ্ট

Debbie Harman

ষ্ট

SYMPHONY OF SOULS

Musical Phantom

Masked is the Lady Phantom
Melodies is the piano opera
Musical is the classical admire
Moving in the shadows of sound
Orchestra is the grand palace Eden

Enchanting by the soul harmony
Halo by voice is so magical gloried
Dancing is the grace by conductor
Musical is her masked phantom heart
By unison in sync emotions masked

Roses Of Redwood

One single Rose by the soil of redwood
Laying by the garden of enchanting beauty
Perfumed is the air in redwood sanctuary
As the cool of the breeze blows a little frisky
Perfect petals all budded together like soft silk

By it's gift of love around with desires embrace
Redwood and it's hoodlum of gorgeous roses
Of purity oh of faith by mirth in nature girth
We hold dear close to soul it is a roses palace
Connected to enjoy Color of simplicity dance

Fresh to the heart as one is placed to the beat
Of the heart by palace of Rose of redwood muse
As the violin is playing to the beauty of the day
By the gates of the redwood palace wonderfully
As one soft pink rose to picked for love by true
Romance blossoming in the garden by scent

Of redwoods roses .
Of redwoods roses

Pretty in the sunlight glowing in the shade
by haze we breathe in it's energy by some
sweet wine of red delight by redwoods palace
violin continues to play so harmonic in the blue
by the soft of the pink roses of courage floret

by redwoods roses
by redwoods roses

By it's gift of love around with desires embrace
Redwood and it's hoodlum of gorgeous roses
Of purity oh of faith by mirth in nature girth

SYMPHONY OF SOULS

We hold dear close to soul it is a roses palace
Connected to enjoy Color of simplicity dance

Of redwoods roses .
Of redwoods roses

Fresh to the heart as one is placed to the beat
Of the heart by palace of Rose of redwood muse
As the violin is playing to the beauty of the day
By the gates of the redwood palace wonderfully
As one soft pink rose to picked for love by true
Romance blossoming in the garden by scent

Of redwoods roses
by redwoods roses

By it's gift of love around with desires embrace
Redwood and it's hoodlum of gorgeous roses
Of purity oh of faith by mirth in nature girth
We hold dear close to soul it is a roses palace
Connected to enjoy Color of simplicity dance

We dance by dance
in the roses of redwood

Roses Of Redwood

Embrace The Wild

Embrace the wild
that we breathe in,
reserve by nature's beauty
it's so wild and wonderfully,
curled into your soul ,

Moved in spirit is the
tiger's pack by wild ,
of run by the roar oh' mighty ,
in passion over the land .

Embrace the wild,
in the jungle of human strong
the heart is in for ride by journey,
holding hands embrace
in with animals wild ,

Moved in the heart is the
triumph in holy earth ,
should rejoice in lagoons
of spring waters of tranquility
bathe in pure majesty

Embrace the wild,
in the greatest power of faith
the soul is emotion in beauty ,
of animals wild and freedom
holding hands embrace ,
in the spirit wild .

Moved in the strength
treasure in light by day/night
the jungle is a animal kingdom
truly colors of brave connect

SYMPHONY OF SOULS

if you just ,

Embrace the wild ,

Truly with heart.

Embrace The Wild

.

Violin Symphony

A orchestra of pure violin
echoing into the morning air ,
as cords spring in sound with heart .

A symphony of grand luxury
mechanical engineer in tradition,   ·
music all good to hear celebrated.

A life of grace in conduct passion
musical in heritage of excite endured,
playing the metal steam punk violin .

A becomes by sweetest symphony
adored for all beauty classic to the soul,
harmony to eternity.

Violin Symphony (steam punk poetry)

Nitro Dreaming

Dreams surface in nitro sleeping mind cocoon
of the very endured astro and faith realm

It makes good connection
circles of simplicity colors and syncs make for
a lovely, tunnels of light neon delight
from the signals of dust and lust
of treasures stones of steam and prediction.

Patterns of love and fate twirl magnetic
around in heart and connections reality,
a atmospheric magic astro, adored and enjoyed into
wildness ...wonderful...something...anything..

It shadow's heart out the fame them, no matter be
things are loved to be treasured in certain ways,
the calm is the faith:emotionally that is cared taken.

By way of life in journey of soul bare, ank look
it choose in faith away, by nitro dream in mind
save it there, and hold close to heart

Nitro Dreaming (Steam Punk Poetry)

❧

Eden Hundsdoerfer

❧

Unknown Journey

to the place i dreamed
so long a time
beyond illusion...for sometime
this shadow of thoughts
in my brain dwelt
time after time wasted
so many questions asked how come

so long my body stagnates
gradually i resign...
identity i can not find
must i trace my origin
thoughts lingered i heard
famous names perhaps am one of them

my guts i gathered
getting into that greyhound
for the east coast bound
counted my last cash...hasted
enough for the bus ride
this man assured things would be good
if i get there....

i wish...i never did
denied me...my very roots
how could he....am shattered
nothing left..my body shivered
cold shoulder....mocked belittled me
heartless and cruel
how could he be

Birkkark Peak

Narrow trail leading towards
maple ground crossing mountain
reaching the other side
we're all surprised by landslide

the trail disappeared suddenly
a man directed new rough
terrain narrow and perilous
looking deep down i avoided
while grasping thick rope

at once i thought could this be
the very end of my existence
God i should not...occupy my mind such
dreadful thoughts my left foot
slipped slightly down
weary and tired but must cross...

still ten minutes away reaching
the safe side of the mountain
i felt dizzy somehow
my feet quivered
held my breathe
my life hung....on that rope

Apricot Valley

i sat beneath...
my eyes feasted....
scenery of paradise
soothed my very soul
breathtaking panorama

firewood on the donkey
immaculate smile.....this girl
her twinkling eyes enchanted
by the early morning hours

at the foot of majestic ranges
icy wind embraced my face
glowing light ....like a door ajar in between
these powerful towering peaks
invaded the spirit within me

in front of me a perfect beauty
apricot fruits gathered by a shepherd
i heard a sweet lovely wine out of these....
the same girl came to me

the next day gave me
a flacon of this delight
savored underneath...
the apricot tree

Bosporus

there lies an ancient city
between east and west
beautiful contrast
historical facts

different beliefs
in harmony lived
traders made fortunes
here starts the orient

euro Asia a great blend
melting pot of both sides
see the magical Topkapi
have you heard of a
flamboyant royal palace

Hagia Sofia impressive
orthodox cathedral
not far the grand blue mosque
distinct ancient landmarks
pride of the Turks

spectacular view
of Bosporus in the midst
where west meets east
this city is at sea
no city so unique
and rich in history than this

The Unknown Land of the Indus

sub-continent there lies this
beautiful land of the pure
dramatic contrast
majestic mountains
northwest frontier

unique landscape
untouched by humans
silk road path of ancient traders
where Marco Polo traversed
with him precious goods and   more

valleys of tranquility
where tube roses a plenty
wild and pretty scented the night
gentle melodious sound
leaves rustled through the night

Sind province there flow
the ancient holy Indus
water of life where falcons
in abundance a rare
type of species

here lies one of the oldest
world civilizations till now
one could see artifacts
rich in heritage and history
so much more to see

Rose Mary McKenzie

Moaning and Groaning

My utterances of Moaning
And groaning came deep from with in
One would come before the other one would end
What is this I feel within my soul
I have no will, I have no control
The day was dark, sky was gray
I heard the evil one say
Come to me, you will see
Just what I have for thee
No!! not me, I did protest
It didn't matter he was on a quest
I will take your life
I won't think twice
You are mine
Your star will not shine
I wept, I sighed
Will someone not take my side?
The gloom was so profound
I fell prostrate on the cold hard ground
Gehenna has sent it hellish hounds
I tried to walk
I tried to run
I knew then, I was undone
I screamed
I yelled
I traveled
Peace did not come
I was in my own private hell
I am fading fast
How long can this torment last
Then, I saw the light of day
I will rescue you I heard Him say
He took my hand

SYMPHONY OF SOULS

He gave me peace
He gave me sweet release
I was lifted up
I did not stay down
I would not be a victim
In Him I am found
I owe my life to this wonderful man
I am on solid rock, not sinking sand
My life is renewed and I give gratitude
All of my days....acknowledging Him always
I am so thankful for all He has done
I live for the Divine   alone
I am the blessed one
God is still on His throne...

The Girl With The Kaleidoscope Eyes

She's tall and young and full of fun
Her smile is like the noon day sun
Eyes are the most beautiful ever seen
Of swirling sea foam green
With on glance she will hypnotize

This girl with the kaleidoscope eye

When this young woman you   meet
You will want to lovingly greet
Looking deep into her soul
If you are so bold
It is with this first glance
You will be under her spell I am told

This girl with the   kaleidoscope eyes

Her beauty was transformed
The day she was born
Heart as big as the sky
Her love is deep and wise

This girl with the kaleidoscope eyes

I love this girl, this woman of mine
Her essence will shine for all time
We have unbreakable ties

This girl with the kaleidoscope eyes

SYMPHONY OF SOULS

Oh, did I mention why she is so dear
Looking at her brought sweet tears
My heart was in her hands
The sun will sets and will rise

On this girl with the kaleidoscope eyes

I love you , please always know
This beautiful grand girl I hold
I am blessed I do confess
She is my prize

This girl with the kaleidoscope eyes

It Is Not Your Time

It is not your time
He said to me eyes smiling so tenderly
But Lord, I'm home to stay!
No, He said, not today
Time to go back home
To live another day
Oh, I saw my Mama, Son, Grandma, brother I looked around
for all the others
They all came running down the hill to me
Such happiness to see
All coming laughing, hugging
What a grand reunion I thought for all eternity
It didn't last was time to go
I felt in my heart, this I did know
It was so simple, yet so profoundly sad
I wanted to stay in Heaven
With my heavenly Dad
I will one day return again
When my life is over
Free from death and pain
I'm looking forward to that day
When He won't say
This is not your time
This is not your day
Our good byes we had to say
He took my hand, walked down the hill
My heard was so happy, it skipped a beat
What a precious thrill
I'm here, alive and well
How I love this time
Etched on my soul and mind
One day He will not say
This is not your time
This is not your day.

Daughter of the Night

I'm a daughter of the night
I walk the street's, in plain sight
I know my game, I'm not ashamed
I have ice running through my veins
I'm a daughter of the night
and you thought I was a good wife
You'd better think about it once or twice
I'm not loving and I not so nice
I'm a daughter of the night
Do wonder why I stay
where the low life gives me pay
The so call love they give to me
is better then any from you I've received
I won't stop, and I won't change
I love my work, I love my game
Here I will stay, now it is you
that must go away
I can't love you any more
I walk the streets, I'm a whore
I'm a daughter of the night
I don't care if it's not right
Can I you entice, love this
daughter of the night...

Liquid Lies

Liquid lies
Hidden in your heart lye's
Spewing out false words
I wish I never heard

Liquid lies
Reach my soul
Pain, heartache unfolds
I fall to my knees
I cease to be

Liquid lies
Hidden deep inside
On the ground in a heap
I don't want to live
Death I seek

Liquid lies
I love you
I touched your heart
You touched mine
Words   evil, not sublime

Liquid lies
Here in the truth
I am falling apart
I have no heart
I have no soul
Death has come
No bells tolled

I have no love
I have no you

SYMPHONY OF SOULS

Now what am I to do

Liquid lies
Liquid lies
I touch your words
They burn like fire
Burning to death

Liquid lies
Turned to stone
Chilling the body, the soul
Heart inflamed
Heart on fire
Liquid lies
Life uninspired

Liquid lies
Unable to hide
No peace can I buy
Now I die...

Billy Charles Root

Homeward

The foot hills encompass all sides
tires hum a familiar travel tune
and the pavement roles out front to rear
as the social sun warms my right arm
and my shades fit just right

There's chaos between the seats
chili peppers on the dial
and the towns along the way fade into mirrored hindsight
the sound of rotating rubber wheres from beneath us

Subterranean desert terrain shrubbery
passes by in green-brown streaks
and my eyes twitch spring loaded left to right recording the
imagery

As we approach a vehicular blockade
of weekend getawayers
we slow and we creep
minutes turn to hours and the miles to
pinpoint map drops

Cajun crawl into the Mojave
the mid day sun is absorbed by dull rock and pebbled sand
and we're in a mountain bowl covered by a laguna blue fade
into blue powder sky cover

On pins and Needles comes the devils armpit of California's
existence
and the next mile marker closes in
as we bridge hover over the Colorado water body flow.

Arizona brings on the evening and the sun transpires into its
daily retire

moonshine emerges from the backstage of cosmic playwrite

The sky darkens and the outer shine of the moon causes a
landscape of shadow's
headlights illuminate otherwise unreadable signs and stripes

As we roll on i see twenty year old memories in my photo
cache mind
i see me and dad
on this same well traveled drive it yourself highway, and I
smile

A fifty mile side trek takes us north to the Paul Bunion pick
fable sight of the grandest of canyons
A wonderful wonder of the seven wonders

In the dark even the most grandest of earthen holes are
invisible
even the great light of night cannot uncover it
and cannot show the depth nor the width
nor length

But, even though the sight be in darkness
a shadow cast in the color of silvery blue caused my soul to
swoon beneath the fullness of the moon

A homeless body lies in sleep only feet from the sharp drop of
this grand earth crack
and we make our way back to the chariot of penske yellow

Early morn brings in a parking lot rest
and the eastern rays awaken us to another roll of day
as the sea of pavement splashes in waves over the hills of the
Arizona desert scape

Rain maker cloud cover pours down upon the flat top
mountains and rock hill's

SYMPHONY OF SOULS

and we saw away at the wheel while robbing the accelerator of all available travel

And the rain cooled wind ricochets off the surrounding skin of our chariot and slaps me around a bit
while high voltage veins fall from the clouds then retract like snapped rubber band's

As we exit the Texas panhandle a red western sunset's behind us
and one more night time black blanket covers us
and the last couple hundred miles become quiet and robotic

The fire from the trail we have blazed is slowly dying into a flicker
Heavy eyes and tightly drawn muscles bring on a dull ache of anxiousness for home

At half past the hour of the new day we end our journey
And home becomes a sweet taste for our road weary soul's
As we finally lay ourselves down for this our long awaited rest.

SYMPHONY OF SOULS

FADED

Thinking of fading away

Into a forgotten cloud of facelessness
Where names are not uttered
And deeds are not seen
Or maybe shrinking down
To the sizeless existence of nothing
Where being unseen is cool
And reflectless images live in mirrors
I guess I could just evaporate
Become a mist unnoticed
Floating carelessly into the moonset
Where molecules separate into atoms and atoms into what was
the question

Thinking about drifting out
Leave me all behind me without me
Just be free from me leaving me
A slow sail over the waves of oneness
I want to pour me out
into a never-ending hole of who and what
Covered by the dirt of who cares
Where hardly a weed would grow
be subtractively negated in willingness
Asunderly tossed and thrown windwise
Wound around an unwinding ringing
blown through airless air unfeathered
If only , IF ONLY
You would be known as knowing is known
If your name would be the only name
Where the sound of it was an eternal vibration of endless
endlessness
If only , IF ONLY
Your face were sought for as diamonds by jewel thieves and

food by the starved
Chased after as the wind chases it own tail and circles endlessly circle
If only you were all that were seen, remembered and chased

John 3 : 30 "He must increase, I must decrease..."

Secluded Notes

I found seclusion
Between ear-budded headphones
They took me to a place of calming drift
Poetry in motion as if a train ride away
Escape momentarily into a small piece
of peace

Eyes close soft and light
While ears absorb the vibes and rhymes
My heart beats within the rhythm
Synchronized with each drum beat
Eye twitches go to steady dark stare

The black and whites come in slow
Cascading tones of finger trickle over the ebony and ivory
keys of soul elsewhere
And I am caught up into the third heaven
Consciousness of where am I
Is eclipsed by acoustic reverberations

like seasonings on sustenance
A salting of steel chords begins mixing
The multitude of coursing sounds Rescue me
Not out of body but out of world
I am present but not wholly here

For the duration of the piece
I am taken away from silence and sound
For all there is , is the music
Strums, beats and taps massage my thoughts
And for a moment
I am one with the vibrations

SYMPHONY OF SOULS

I am the bass drums hollow holler
I am the pickups of electrified six strings
I am the blending of the piano keys
I am become the music...

SYMPHONY OF SOULS

Demon's Breath

Demon's breath
upon my neck
The sin within caress

Rebirthing memory
of yester-gone days
Reflections of the wretch

Festering gaze
of evil ways
How I was back when

Refreshing the deeds
the growth of demon seeds
Pig in the mire splashing around in sin

Tongue flicker against my lobe
Deadman plans glittery strobe
my ear begins to itch

Sound of desire
Lustful fire
Unwanted but still I twitch

A loss of me
Is all I see
Demons laugh in my ear

Mind on fire
Brow perspire
Drown within my fear

Dark no sight
Soul in plight
See a candle burn

Stare full forward
Eyes on flame and word
Slowly I turn

Translucent patterns of thought and time
Wash out the dirty feet of my mind
Now I see you for what you truly are
Now I reach for the bright morning star

Come to my rescue
take me away
Nothing more the demon can say

With shivers he leaves me
Into the shadows he goes
The light now with me
I fear no more foes

SYMPHONY OF SOULS

Mirror Mirror

Mirror mirror on the ground
how many your shards
on floor be found
Shattered about
the bed room surround
Mirror mirror on the ground

Broken mirror all over the place
who has broken
your most beautiful face
Don't tell no lies
for you know it was I
who threw you from
your resting grace.

A deceivers reflection
you showed to me
which was a monster
I refuse to be
What's on the surface
is all you see
I cannot be
what you show me to be

You showed me an image
of unrighteousness
Stained up tinted black
with the Devils kiss

You showed me an image
of callousness
And a harden heart
with demons hiss

Mirror mirror
on table and chair
where you shattered
when I threw you there

I shattered your lying
Sight reflect
When you showed me an image
of a sinful wreck

I cannot believe this
as a truth to be
For you only showed an image
of the outer me
And that is not
my true identity

Look into my eyes
with your silvery lies
But still you cannot see
with in me
and so no good
will you find

you cannot see
what I'm thinking
You cannot reflect
my heart
And that is why I broke you
to tear my failed identity to shards

Mirror mirror
Who's laughing now
You showed me a picture
of a jester clown

SYMPHONY OF SOULS

So I took you from up high
and threw you down
Scattered you far and neigh
And broke the frown

With a pan and broom
I will sweep you away
Throw you out
for you have no more to say...

Olfa Drid

Inner Struggle

Satan:
Hey unlucky you...self-image, so poor?
Style? Face? Erogenous zones need cure?
God's imperfect...got bad allure...
Ugly nose? Lips? Obesity? How endure?
Plastic surgery...best solution for sure...
More preys...let's tempt and lure...lure...lure...

God:
Thou, wise and patient creatures
I am the one and only one Creator
I am the universe and human Initiator
I am thy bones and flesh Maker
Designed thee all special and unique!
Fancy similar items in the same boutique?

Satan:
Hey ugly males and females,
Find faces unappealing? Repelling?
Feel frustrated? Unloved? Revolting?
Flesh...flesh...secret... easy job...
Strip-teasers...become kings...queens...
Shut...shut rooms...behind PC screens...
Private webcams...nothing done...nothing seen...
Loads of lovers...lovers...display your beauty...
Damned era...no jobs...this job is your duty ...duty...duty...

God:
Thou, honest and loyal followers
My divine camera is forever shooting thee
All thy secret deeds and even secret thoughts
My angels are penning all thy shots and faults

SYMPHONY OF SOULS

Satan:

Hey fantastic...powerful rich men
Bombastic words...diamonds...cars...Viagra pills,
Fame...sexy...cute babes... all at your knees will...
Merchandise...merchandise...rife...don't miss the deal...
Condom in pocket... phantasms...phantasms fill...fill... fill

God:

Thou, men of wealth and faith
Thy property is my gift to thee
It shall be thy test and also thy key
Cater for thy family and why not amuse
Keep them in no need, and pay thy dues
Thy parents and the needy, with gifts shower
Wealth is no money, property or power
Wealth is gratitude, pity and generosity
Kindness, correctness and modesty

Satan:

Hey...hey buddies...feel helpless? Hopeless?
Wanna forget stress? Frequent pitfalls?
Come...come...gulp beer...alcohol...
Best medicine ...for aches...aches all...
Taste hash...cannabis or marijuana...
Join me in heaven...heaven...don't you
wanna?...wanna?...wanna?

God:

Ignorant if to him sell thy brain gift
To emptiness and loss, thou will drift
Never ever taste drug and alcohol
To his puppets, he shall reduce thee all!
Be pious, moral, awake and aware
Inner and outer peace, feel and share

Satan:

Insatiable senses…senses…break fences…
Ears...tongue...touch…sight… smell…
Follow…follow them…find pretenses
Satisfy…satisfy them... in all tenses…tenses...tenses...

God:

Thy senses are doors for him to enter
In thy luxurious 5-star-body he wants to shelter
Thy acts, mood and speech, he yearns to mentor
Do not place him at thy life's center
Of my Holy book, be forever a hunter

Satan:

Hey stubborn… strong…strong fellows…
To your good…correct…right opinions glue…
Let no one argue…contend…challenge you…
Never open minds for a different view…view… view…

God:

Thou, children of Adam and Eve
Satan, thy enemy, made thee his dollies
All his adverts and oaths are but follies
To drag thee, he intends to his fake bazaar
All his goods, sales and bargains are that bizarre
How come in his stores and malls shop so far?
Your human worth reduced all to a single dinar...

No More Violence

Violence has
no color
no religion
no caste
no gender
no race

Violence emanates from
the soulless
the wicked
the rotten
the savage
the cruel
the hostile
the egocentric &
the barbaric,
whose hearts
for mercy and
for the 'Other'
left   no place

Violence is the offspring of evil
evil is the rival of good
good and evil are inherent in
the Jewish
the Christian
the Muslim
the Atheist
the Buddhist
and also in the 'chameleons'
with more than one face
Violence gives birth to

hate
hurt
aggression
murder
assassination
annihilation
and entails nothing but
an un-erasable trace

Violence should be
repudiated and abated
in each corner of the globe
wherever it slyly sneaks
looking   for a permanent
identity and place

So,
Halt to violence !
Halt no bloodshed !
Halt to racism !
Halt to fanaticism !
Halt to terrorism !
Halt to barbarism !
Halt to war!

Let's cure ourselves
from WITHIN and tame this
shameful trait belonging to
the human /inhuman race...

BELOVED (...)

as soon as I wake up
I think about you
feel like to hold you
feel like to touch you...

as soon as I remember you,
I forget my family,
my parents
my spouse
my kids
my duties
my hunger
my needs...
my real name...

as soon as I get in touch with you,
the whole world is brought to its knees:
the farthest ones come close,
the oldest friends   reemerge,
the inaccessible things become accessible,
the unfathomable concepts become fathomable,
the buried dreams are resurrected,
the unknown folk become famous,
the unspeakable topics are spoken,
the alleged taboo is broken
the silenced opinions are voiced
the past memories are recalled
the adults are rejuvenated
the young are given wings to fly
the locked doors are unlocked
the frontiers are trespassed...

as soon as I lose touch with you,

I feel lonely,
displaced,
misunderstood,
abandoned,
confused,
heartbroken
disconnected…

how spellbinding your love is!

You're made out of metal with
no flesh
no bones
no heart
no senses
no mind
no soul

Still…

have such power to overwhelm
all humans with your love…

in this crazy era, no one can ever deny
his addictive love to you: dear PC !

Time Ravages

Midway amid my dawn and dusk
Time knocked on my heart's door
blowing a gentle breeze of musk
to perfume my stinky core

Replied that brave 'i' in me: why
shall you repent a death
which made me touch the seventh sky?
take a bow for holding my breath
and for uplifting my soul high

Oh Time, just go by
needn't brake to apologize!
Hadn't it been for your doom
which for Poetry made room,
I wouldn't have learned how
to transcend gloom
and be ready again to bloom.

Love Mystery

O Love, who are you ?
why do all humans yearn for your tender touch?
are you a seed of a flower in our fertile hearts to grow ?
a blazing fire, our senses to burn ?
a morning fog, our vision to blur ?
a touch of madness, our reason to blind?
a colonizer, in our senses to settle?
a vampire, our blood to suck?
a chain, our freedom to restrain?
a tornado, our minds to blow?
a magnet, our desires to hypnotize?
a shooting star, to show up then wane so far   ?

how do your victims look like
after embracing your Majesty?
reasonable or crazy ?
shielded or vulnerable ?
realist or idealist ?
sober or drunk?
sublime or pathetic ?
hollow or complete ?
masters or slaves ?
leaders or followers ?
lions or lambs ?
free birds or caged ones ?
which emotions do you fuel in them ?
delight and ecstasy ?
longing and bliss ?
pleasure and desire ?
belongingness and possessiveness?
jealousy and craziness?
togetherness and wholeness ?
what are they liable to commit for your sake?

SYMPHONY OF SOULS

blunders?
follies?
homicides?
suicides?

how do they feel in your absence?
paralyzed?
mutilated?
uprooted?
empty?
wingless?
pointless?
aimless?

what if you betray your devotees?
won't you metamorphose into a criminal?
masochist and untrustworthy ?
liar and manipulator ?
heartbreaker and murderer ?
hypnotist and illusionist ?

why are we then allowing ourselves to be
consumed and inhaled,
swallowed and devoured by you?
why are you that
dangerous yet irresistible ?
untamable yet adoptable?
unfathomable yet desirable?
invincible yet challengeable?
insatiable yet incomparable ?

still and against all odds,
when animosity prevails, you're the one we conjure…
when danger looms in the horizon, you are the one we hug …
when conflicts overwhelm us, you're the one we resurrect…
when emotions are barren, you're the one to emerge…
when darkness reigns, you're the one to shine…

SYMPHONY OF SOULS

when all else perish, you are the one to cherish…

paradoxically enough, even
when you break us into pieces, some still trust you…
when you annihilate us , some still long for your slaps …
when you pain us, some still enjoy your suffering…
when your fire burns us, some still caress your entailed
scars…
when you chain our souls, we adore our enslavement to you…
when you are erased, your trace remains engraved in our
hearts …

who on earth can ever claim to be
as universal as you!
as risky as you!
as omnipresent as you !
you have that grace to intrude in every heart,
in every house,
in every community,
in every nation ,
in all nations ,
in different nations,
using the same guile and guts, yet
no one soever has dared to condemn you
for your abrupt intrusion!

you are such an undefinable entity with that
magic power to trespass all physical and
metaphysical frontiers
and end up being treasured and
welcomed too, and
we, poor humans,
can't help being trapped by you!

all humans of all cultures and
through the ages have tried
to decipher your mystery

SYMPHONY OF SOULS

but in vain…
yet, they have all agreed at least
upon your enchanting weirdness
upon your puzzling paradox
upon your tempting ravages
upon your bewitching absurdity
and
upon the voidness of life without you…

❧

Dennis John Ferado

❧

SAD EYES

Our dreams are like ashes they blow in the breeze
We chase after quickly with one life to leave
I know you from somewhere your smile has no schemes
It sure wasn't heaven it must be my dreams
Perhaps a warm morning so golden and fine
Did I stumble to you all drunken and blind
Did you stretch out your arms to take me inside
Did you give me your love and then let me hide
The hard ways of this world are wicked and wise
And all of its sadness lies deep in your eyes
Did I come to you screaming out of the night
Did you quiet my crying make it all right
Ideas are like pictures that hang up to float
We watch them go by as they go up in smoke
Did I take it for granted your love to keep
When you wiped my brow and then rocked me to sleep
The tattered hand of winter smacks at my cheek
The wind-swept snow covers up my frozen feet
Will I see you again like birds from the south
Will I see your sad eyes or kiss your warm mouth

Sad eyes my mind keeps trying..
Sad eyes my heart keeps dying...

I WONDER:

At the mysteries of the universe,
I marvel at the infinite possibilities of the soul,
The endless tributaries and rivulets churning
In one lifetime and the choices we are tortured with;
I am bamboozled by the secrets in the animals eyes,
Souls who yearn to speak; I am mystified by the
Miraculous trees their song is strong and moves my
Foundation, I am lightning struck, awed by acts of
Natures unmatched fury and resistant forces; I am
Boggled by a living earth who gives us everything
we

Need as we antagonize, poison and torch it--yet it
Endures--I am amazed by every living thing and its
Individuality, the planets in their mathematical paths,
The sun who gives us life, the moon who moves the
Waters, the geometrical coordination of organic
matter,

As I walk past myself.

ME AND JIM
(back in '63)

in a twisting rivulet flowing to the west
I'm swimming backwards through the current of a time
when the hour glass was only just beginning
we went speeding through dimensions of adventure
a squall of boisterous youth and anticipation
burdened with the hunger of two ravenous wolves
walked barefooted over hill 'cross Polk and Geary
sky marbled with pink clouds above the orange bridge
hooting at the moon we ran with Johnny Cortez
only two possessions enchantment and unrest
servants of confusion but, hey, what did we care
singing in the streets "as long as she needs me" and
"I left my heart where those little cable cars climb...,"
searching for some rapture all day and all night too
thirty days of teeming rain till the sun broke through
and never really giving up our tenancy
but always, just barely, escaping from the flood
even though gifted with excessive senselessness
we swallowed San Francisco like bubbly champagne

Did you ever have the feeling that you were being watched?

Sometimes I get that feeling...

I AM THE ONE

I am the rain that quenches your thirst
The poem that you studied and rehearsed
I am the hunger of the lost hound
I am the stones that hold you earthbound
I am the damp grass between your toes
I am the meadow where you run free
I am the echo in a grand hall
I am the singing bells when they toll
I am the oak of great dignity
I am the leaf that withers and falls
I am the One
I was the mountain where you now stand
Now I'm that rock beaten into sand
I am the tree with whom you ponder
I am that eagle with whom you fly
I am the friend with whom you wander
I am the dew that clings to your lips
I am the snake that crawls in the pits
I am the dust that gusts in your eyes
I am sensations hidden inside
Think you feel somebody by your side
I am the One
I am the strings in your rhapsody
I am the sea that streams through your veins
I am the root of your melody
I am the doorway into your mind
I am candles that gleam in your eyes
I am the twilight forever young
I am the song that cleaves to your tongue
I am the wind that lashes your face
Steals your breath lifts up that dress of lace
I am the space where the stars are strung
I am the One.

SYMPHONY OF SOULS

I am the walk you take in the sky
I am the cloud you rest on to sigh
The crack of the daybreak when you wake
Obsidian black seen when you sleep
I am the sheen that lives in your hair
I am the breezes you hear that speak
I am the blush that colors your cheeks
I am the branches starting to creak
When   the trees are all frozen and bare
When you think that you sense someone there
I am the One..

NEW YORK CITY SONG

Tight rope walkers, city stalkers
Come to meet you come to greet you
With the morning sun days begun
In New York City.
Skinny ladies, hairline crazies
Push and shove as they live and love
In downtown's zone, right off Great Jones
In New York City.

Heat so hot around mid July
Chill so cold from a wintry sky
Spring and fall sheer beauty behold
In New York City.
Buildings high dance with rolling skies
Sing with sadness, ring with gladness
It's evening time I'm feeling fine
In New York City.

Taxi drivers, thieves and liars,
Beggars sinners, would-be winners,
Creeps and clowns all hanging around
In New York City.
Big time boppers, city hoppers,
Wealthy women chauffeur driven
Run around in a rich man's town
In New York City.

Through many days of wind and rain
I'm different now I'm not the same.
Get so tired of ties that bind
I'm the one always running blind
From head to toe my name's not mine
In New York City.

SYMPHONY OF SOULS

David Hall

At the Fair

Daddy bought tickets and some cotton candy
From a man, Mr. YankeeDoodleDandy
I had never tasted cotton candy before
That first bite had me coming back for more

I saw Mr. IrishWarrior with red beard and kilt
And Mr. ReallyLongLegs juggling stuff on stilts
I laughed out loud at Mr. Midget running around
Being chased down by Mrs. Policewoman clown

I jumped when I saw flames shoot into the air
Mr. FlameThrower had my full attention there
Then Mrs. SwordSwallower showed up
The cotton candy dropped and I upchucked

Daddy laughed, holding my hand, we walked away
Telling me how it happened to him the same way
"Really?" I asked.   Squeezing his big hand tight
Smiling, confident we walked on into the night

Then I saw the beautiful multi-colored Ferris wheel
Soon we were stopped on the very top, what a thrill
He pointed out our house, church and school
Man, you could see forever, this was so cool

We rode the teacups and squealed with delight
Rode some other rides full of flashing lights
We laughed and had fun everywhere we went
We even sneaked and peed behind the tiger tent

With the wonder of a tired child in my eyes
I stared at the bursting fireworks in the skies
I felt his strong hand tussling my hair
Me and MY daddy at the fair…

In the Storm

Outside, an icy wind blows
whipping
rustling
through the dried trees
oaken branches claw at this ancient house.

Inside, the candles flames
dance and sway
under the whim
of whistling drafts.

Thunder booms
as if in symphony
with the creaks
and groans
of this house's old bones.

I sit at the weathered upright
fingers delicately
tinkling on its stained ivories
and play a song
from yesteryear.

Calmly enjoying
my moment in the storm.

Realm of Shadows

I walk not alone but in solitude here in the realm of shadows
Hating the feeling of the warm blood dripping from my hands
Wondering what cruel fate cast me such strange bedfellows?
Hoping against hope to return to my love in my homelands

These lips have tasted gore today as fierce the battles were
fought
Salty sweat mixed with bits of the enemy's blood and bone
The horrors that these eyes have seen; what hath man wrought
I fear the scars outside will heal long before the inner ones are
gone

The envelope of night brings with it a small measure of relief
For somewhere in the infinite darkness lies a path of escape
For in the core of mind untouchable lies the truth of my belief
In the realm of shadows, snatched moments in dreams take
shape

In the realm of shadows through dreams once again we meet
There the golden sunlight softly caresses and frames your face
Roaring thunder of many drums is only my pounding
heartbeat
But then the cruel mornings cry rips me from my sacred place

The enemy has been spotted massing for an early morning
attack
The various strangers that surround me quickly leap to their
arms
With shining steel we prepare to drive the enemy strangers
back
Soon even the inner sentries are sounding their panicked
alarms

SYMPHONY OF SOULS

I walk in solitude into another battle against the realm of
shadows
These battles must be fought the victory with our blood
bought
This evil enemy of ours has been delivered some serious
blows
They must be completely defeated or I fear it will be for
naught

I fight not for the kings or noblemen nor banners flapping in
the wind
The memories of returning from the hunt to find my family
dead
Sears me, drives me, burns me like a candle flaming at both
ends
Blood will drip red from my sword as the hatred roars in my
head

I fight with the passion of a soulless one that is not afraid to
die
I leap to the forefront, hungry for revenge and the taste of
death
Fire pounding, raging through my veins, and bloodlust in my
eye
My family will be avenged, this I swear until my dying breath

I yearn for the heat, stench and sweat of battles fiercely fought
The spray of the vile ones blood and the crunch of their bone
I also ache for my eternal deliverance to be finally bought
When the last enemy is dead and to hell their souls have gone

Then the welcome embrace of death would be such a relief
The unknown journey into the afterlife could finally start
Firm and strong, I will hold onto this my ultimate belief
I'll follow the path of the pounding drums in my heart

To be reunited with my love, my one and only, my wife

SYMPHONY OF SOULS

There we will walk hand in hand in the golden sunlight
Tasting a sweetness of love greater than one of mortal life
An eternity of immortals with wings of angels taking flight

The agony of this world will no longer be our tether
In the realm of light and eternity, we'll enjoy our forever

I Pushed the Dark Door Open

I pushed open a dark door
the light bled into dimly lit bar
the barkeep nods a silent welcome.
"Give me a double shot of Crown" I tell him
though he already knows.
I savor the burning
as the whiskey ignites the flames
that carve out the remnants of my sanity.
Memories start to dance through my mind
like flames upon old dried wood.
The barkeep sets up another double
a bowl of peanuts
and a small white napkin.
He lingers for a second
but I have no interest in idle chatter
the fire inside dances higher
and it brings more memories to the party.
But only one memory matters.
I hear her voice
the only voice that I will ever heed.
Oh to hear the velvet in that voice
one more time.
But it can never be.
Slamming the empty glass down, I say
"Bartender! Another!"
As he calls me a cab
a scoundrel in the mirror
is mocking me
that ole drunken sot.
Have I lost my Queen or gained a Crown
And I pushed the dark door open.

Real Men Wear Pink

Real Men Wear Pink

She walked in and slowly closed the door
My team was playing on the TV
I was fully into the game
But I felt a change in the air around me
I grabbed the remote and muted the sound
I watched her hand lingering on the door
Head down, keys dangling she stood
My eyes furrowed and my feet hit the floor
"Honey, are you okay?"
"What's the matter?
I crossed over to her
Into my arms she crashed
My mind was racing like crazy
"What is going on I asked softly?"
To the couch I carried my lady
Heart wrenching sobs racked her body
Mascara and makeup ran down her face
Clumsily I tried to wipe it away with my shirt
I'm a man; I just made a bigger mess all over the place
Oh how I wish I could take away her hurt
She cried on into the night
And for hours I knew not why
I cried there with her cause I loved her and it was my right
We cried till our eyes were dry
Then she kissed me so tenderly
And we made sweet love
After the passion she told me softly
About the cancer the doctor had told her about
I saw all the fears in her eyes
I saw all the worry and the self doubt

SYMPHONY OF SOULS

I couldn't begin to fathom them all
But one I could help her realize
Everything else seemed so insignificant and small
Locked in embrace, I looked into her eyes
I let her see my soul
As in the day we wed
I gave my instincts full control
And let her hear what my heart said
I placed her hand over my heart
"In sickness and in health
For better or worse
Richer or poorer
Till death do us part"

Ten years later

She walked in and slowly closed the door
I sit here watching my game
I watch her walk across the floor
I'm the wood, she's the match, and we are flame
I see her curled up reading her book
Things have never been the same
She looks up, smiles and gives me that look
I love her unabashedly with acclaim
So proud of the woman she became
So impressed of all she overcame
So in awe of that look that so quickly can inflame
When they ask me if I can wear pink
To support the breast cancer cause
I don't even have to think
I answer without a pause
Yes, because we all know a lady
That is a daughter or a mother
A sister or a lover
A survivor and a fighter

SYMPHONY OF SOULS

Maybe a lady
That's crossed over to the other side
I bow my head and pray
That we can defeat this evil
And save our ladies this day

❧

Margaret Gudkov

❧

Once upon a time in "Dolce vita"

Once upon a time
My life was simply "Dolce vita"
Did not mean bathing in the fountain of Trevi
In front of the admirers in ballgown , no such episode

I came too close personify Anita Ekberg
Running through the streets of Rome in complete
abandon
Immersed in the world I build in my imagination
Magical, bohemian retreat where troubles don't belong

Loving the carelessness, bundles of attention
Changing the lovers way one change the gloves
The international array , served on the plates
The mix of cultures doused with spicy dressing

Rome, Venice, Florence, New York
Spending time, spending the funds
Refusing not , whatever Lola wants ,Lola gets
No question, train left the station in the while, wake up
call

Adagio

The leaves staccato in midair
Embraced by the wind eternal evolution
Falling on top of each other in the graceful garland
Whispering somber "Adagio" to ears of whoever want to
listen

Last ball the nature gives before the winter
Clearly I hear the notes striped of cheerful notoriety of
summer
Autumnal hues calling for a smile, sad smile of forgiving
Forgetting things, forgetting people hurt you with
Incapacity of feelings , callous shadows

Burgundy veined leaf unwittingly touched my arm
As if old friend reminding me to shake off melancholy
So intricate design impressed on it's face
You wonder how simple things could be so perfect
So divine in such small scale,off he flew away
"Adagio" Vivaldi played softly , fitting well the scene

Sugar on the Lips

Give me the sugar on the lips
Mmm, the divine concoction
Mixing of chocolate with a whipped cream
Can't get enough, continuously licking mouth

Espresso,cappuccino flowing in the steaming river
Filling whole body with a captivating aura
Not feeling drops of rain , nor cooling touch of
snowflakes
The magic carpet taking you to the exotic islands

My lips, weathered and dry
Suddenly transforming into voluptuous organ
Doughy, mushy,comfy pillows you lay your lips on
Resting in complacent laziness of pleasure

Another day in Life

Another day in life
Not really different from one before him
The monotony of the job , tedious rides
Pushing to get things done, forgetting yourself

In evening laying on the bed in meditative mood
Remembering the course, tallying mistakes
Finding there no sense in running such a marathon
Imagining to be far from the meddling crowds

Oh how cold, the back in shivering frustration
Yearning for hugs, for cuddling in the front of TV
The nights are worst to get through, wishing for the
mornings
Bringing the light , the hope to find the love, true love
If that exist at all

Don't Stare

Don't stare, you seen the nakedness before
Are other women any different from me?
Standing bare, devoid of false make up
Eve never wore the costume either , meeting Adam

Your eyes are glued, what separate me from
Females, paraded through the stages of the life
Thick thighs, thin waists, blondes or brunettes
Good sex or boring like routine of satisfaction

They left the premises , but I am here now
Modeling myself , not the designer dress
The nakedness is natural to humans since living in the
caves
Only later the decency dictated wearing costumes on the
public

Yet before the lover is not matter
I gift you my most prized possession
Exposing all, help yourself, be gentle wind
Filling innards with the pleasure, carrying to Eden
My nakedness in body and the thoughts is yours
We came full circle , back to where love began
Becoming yourselves Adam and Eve

SYMPHONY OF SOULS

Debbie Rice

Broken'thoughts

Flying upon the wings and will of foolish aspirations, with
sparkling eyes of everlasting promise, hanging on every word
and worship of every syllable, plunged into reverie and let the
self be stranded in sugar-coated looking-glass,

dreams blind to the catatonic cacophony hidden beneath and
within the seductive symphonies, the heart and mind have lost
each other. 'Til, there are no more words between mouth and
soul.

But it calls softly to the sleepwalking enchanted marionette,
the faint whispers reaching wooden ears incomprehensible,
indiscernible, and imperceptible with the lingering silent
nothings that drown the fading voices,

an utterance of heartfelt stumbling yet nowhere near enough,
And yet still it demands. The inability to whisper anything or
express self, the fleeting glimpses into the hearts essence.

Dismayed the memories swirled with absolute momentum.
Bubbles bursting with vibrant camber in all dynamic fractals,
stray thoughts turn into incipient concentration with such
discordant noises.

The chasms of emotions drawn into a spiral spin and petals of
being falling carelessly aside like leaves in a blackened wind.
Harshness and reality stinging the skin with needles of misery
and turmoil participating heartily in it, the illusion arises
maintaining this isolation.

The web closes in, enveloping all around, caressing the mind
in all its corners. The voids of time with its long tendrils grasp

SYMPHONY OF SOULS

the legacy of space as it is sucked into oblivion.

Despair cries out in that moment of stillness and yet it is met with effortless motion of kaleidoscopic colors, silent tapers of light swaying, dancing within the echoes of the past.

There is something more substantial needed not the coercive tug of harsh norms nor the fleeting disharmony reigning absurdity,

nor the gentle pressure of indescribable tension upon the heartstrings stemming taut from the deadened material that comprises the mind and not played upon like the nylon of the beaten un-tuned guitar.

The wish is that it would speak out bluntly for once rather than lacing each muted word with acoustics of deliberate ambiguity that has brought with it disorder and discord,

sing out clearly with its rumbling bass lines deep and smooth without distortion, resonating stronger than each cadence of the pulsing rhythmic organ, to rouse the cranium from narcotic stupor that is ensuring instability.

Produce mental mobility and set the hammering forks of the atrium on tuned trumpeting frequency for the perfect melody.

The inner sigh follows, finally rests on the surface of the mind.

SYMPHONY OF SOULS

THROUGH THE VEIL...

Upwards the soul of spirit glides through a darkened
emptiness and on through twists and turns of the spinning
vortex,
spanning the rifts of inner space and embroidered by the
radiant needle of an ethereal spell– far within the weaving
patterned trails of magnificence from fractal dazzling arcs.
Like a metamorphic hand they reach out, of their own
brilliance, encircling ripples and rotating softly through a
reverie they merge with more illusions,
rhythmical tempestuous ballet of tenderly entwined embrace,
an elegant breeze of flamboyant symbols and spheres of
eternal music – whom do not lack syllables nor rhyme.
Forever onward through whirling flushing suffusions,
blushing like crimson-tipped rosettes of flame,
passing through arches of gold and silver, curving through
time like celestial bow,
and on through the crystalline crescents with tall silver
dendroid's gleaming, the astral rainbows spangled spurs
casting a multi-hued shadow of light upon a whispered reality.
Lost into a world of symphonic power and reflecting
emotional shaded translucence, a labyrinth of thoughts
showering color in luminescent of flight.
Forever in vivid crescendos, bursting asunder as an arrow of
light with a target of absolute aim, flowing like fountains
through moon-lit skies, swiftly ascending in bright silver
spirals – sparkling like frozen crystal diamonds in
star-showered eyes,
headlong the soul soars through this actuated spectrum,
spraying forth snowflakes of tear-shattered moonbeams
–rocketing outwards in shimmering aurorae, pulsating in
fragile streams filling the heavens with glistening haze.
The carousel of the celestial, immortals –who passes ever,
through 'prism gate' eternal portal, to other world concealed

SYMPHONY OF SOULS

from all like an iridescent stream of ghostly chimes,
energy twisting and spinning as an turbulent musical dance
passing to new dimension allowed by sentinels of light and
time,
enchantments of a route obscure within boundless chasms,
unblemished without form and no man can discover.
The winds of words breathe and spirits whisper murmured
echoes, till all receive that Incandescent call

SYMPHONY OF SOULS

Chorale of Coral

Coral sea dreaming in liquid abstractions, to the beat of an eye
Whispering tendrils flounce a pattern, spiraling sound to the
sky
Bursting tartan melody infused within harmony creating
amaze
Reflecting on pink water beads of fuchsia flapping in the
haze,

Labyrinth branches of golden strings strumming quite laden
Symmetric gravity surrounded by a rotating baroque garden
A kaleidoscopic song in finite crystal dust granting it pardon

Clouds mounting on the fusion, breaking thru t'is the galaxy,
Echoed waves of velvet bellow spring prisms bright and
waxy
Drawing parched feathery orbs and dusty orange
globe-mallows,
Soft explosion of Smokey amber tones twirling like
swallows

Collide in star splashed floral dance catching halo to the
vision
And blazed chorale tempest in a wing of raspberry caped
fusion
Satin moons caress the vibration in to fluorescent symbolic
flight
The velvet flowing embers traces chocolate snowy flames of
light

A fractal carnival crackles a feast, like dreams upon a circus
wall
Ballistic rainbow skyscrapers of symbol arc touch senses

SYMPHONY OF SOULS

then call
Golden brilliance of water-bubbles tender ballet, spread
melody tall

Placid butterfly factions coil decorative shadows of blushing
eclipse
The infinite insignia and bliss within a glittering flux of
dusky tender lips
Sweet blue plateau of carpet jingle bulbs stream laughingly
across the floor
Tuneful charade, a visual opera and assortment of vibrant
choir at the door

Fruitful abound, delicate fragrance tones vibrantly crowned
in bouncing blue
In all this triangular luminaire of treasure, a fluttering energy
world of iridescent hue
Beauteous pleasure…the heard shades, musical tones and
pattern for me.. it is true

SYMPHONY OF SOULS

Indwelling multi-sensory treasure of seeing beyond what is perceived …. A metaphoric hand of 'curse' or 'gift'

Cranial fireworks synched with life's aural soundtrack create
striking patterns, surrounded by an electric dance of light that
portray musical compositions,
every instrumental voice has a different shape and pulsating
with a groovy rhythm of color manipulating flight and sound.
Clouds of scintillating fractals; riding twisting waves that
virtually crackle with pictographic energy,
vividly powerful depiction of tones and atmospheric ethos
becoming graphic ciphers expressed emotions within the
spectrum.
Within these, the sparks of flashing symbolic rays, charged
with stimulating tension that grows exponentially into infinity,
yet remaining constant in value, forms a repeating mosaic
separated by vibrant scale.
Mystically glowing the glistening dew essence sky, listening
and seeing repeating verses like a tender caressing serenade,
set to tune and strummed with silken satin within the natural
luminescence,
the aura pulsates in time to the flowing blood veins within
the land, achieving that lyric simultaneity and embodies the
abstract sound patterns of choral voices, of gentle instruments
performing an vibrant orchestra.
The allusion to music is strengthened by the rhythmic
interplay of streaks, patterns and forms. Expressed in tangible
constants fixed by strata and composition,
the fusing of the most elemental design create sound fluidly,
sashaying the imaginary into existence assures the turbulent
mind of incessant curiosity that darkness, holds beauty of
which many cannot fathom.
The enigmatic, with a wide beautiful array of colors passing
through the ears, music dramatically shifting like a beautiful

being with fiery numbers,
a poetically chaotic equation, the integrated transcendent
experience so mysterious, beautiful frenetic and vaguely sad,
subtle ever-changing expressions of vivid decorated voices
and angry frustrated calculations are all too natural.
The momentum strides forward, surpassing the limits of the
body; it ripples outward in curving and streamlined ribbons, as
if molded by the aerodynamic of its passing.
There is a feeling of vitality and pulsing rhythm; horizontal
divisions of soft floating sphered spaces are an invitation to
enter into the depth of, and to become totally saturated with
and around, as if the alignment is meant to resemble a dancing
masterpiece,
within the dynamic contrast of antagonisms, a resonant
relationship is constructed between optical vibration and
energetic visual music.
The energy-laced appearance of many landscapes and visual
depictions of sounds, vibrant colors, edgy shapes, and
energized scale illuminated by a surreal light, a living surface,
the image presents a metamorphose —a morphing of meaning.
The undefined background envelops and evokes a numinous
feeling of infinity with an almost breathing energy, within the
luminous quality; the streamlined shades seem to move back
and forth, giving form as another living presence.
The vagueness and ambiguity, the merging forces, fragments
of subjection with bounds, reflects a desire to go beyond,
remembering from both sides with such intensity causes the
eye to think in a completely different way, creates multiple
ways of seeing things simultaneously....the impossible in the
possible..

SYMPHONY OF SOULS

Symphony of Silence

SILENCE' many a musical wave, streams of patterns dancing
with luxurious florescence, a magical union, shrouding and
canopying all aspects in floral profusion.
Resonant with vibrations, the unique scented verses within
like an intangible embodiment in the land of illuminated
imagination.
The soul exists and sways caressed with gentle embrace as
silence plays and sings its colorful lullaby entwining the entire
being.
Beautiful rhythm and imagery, it inculcates an extreme
essence to fasten together, the unspoken truth awareness,
abstract stillness intriguing but also opaque, a calmness in
euphoric glory melodiousness within and around.
And softly silence speaks..... Hear the rhythmic eloquent
sound, muse of flow relentless and efficient in purpose,
everlasting amid serene calmness forever enchanted by a
maelstrom of psychedelic resonance seeking within.
And whispered within in the sounds of hush, a cacophony
through which your soul exquisitely tortured, disturbing
dynamics of diabolic weird and wonderful designs, filling the
whole ambience, beautiful deep expression of calm intoned,
thus stillness be the painter…inside the within…a greater
creative, swept up in the myriad of sound and symbols,
textures and color, bubbles of subconscious, of synthesis and
its cathartic creation…. to get lost, if only momentarily, in the
sweet symphony that is silence... .
Captivating leading, this succulent tranquility makes the
mind wonder and wander, comes alive with visions not to be
uttered as one takes the journey into that realm,
access pure potentiality in dimensions of peace, aid mental
spiritual perception, too full of wisdom for the tongue of
profound experiences to utter it in mere words, intelligible to
others maybe, perhaps, cannot explain it, though be

misunderstood for it.
Drowned ever in unsolved and bizarre enigma; stunned by
the celestial sculptors of reality.
Yet I cast aside turmoil, this burst of thought; to the echoes
and entrails of dreams, in the silence of mind, predestined path
as revealed,

the reverberating exotic patterns of surreal wind fills the void,
forever find time to experience my silence.

SYMPHONY OF SOULS

❧

Joe Wilson

❧

It shouldn't be this way...

Our journey is one that's fraught with danger
In decisions oft our choices make us doubt
But right to our final breath and from the manger
Guidance from our parents should help us out.
Oft-times we think ourselves alone.
The pain we feel can break us into pieces
With wreckage of us strewn across the floor
A gathering sense of wrong creates the creases
Of a life that doesn't want to breathe any more.
Oft-times we think ourselves alone.
Late at night when shadows begin their taunting
And the world will close itself behind locked doors
Is the time when sorrow begs the most affection
It's always someone's fault, even mine or yours.
Oft-times we really are alone.

A Golden Thread...

A golden thread runs through my life
it keeps me safe with warmest love
along the way this well fit glove
has helped me live when I might not
when if I died meant not a jot
caring always that I'm well
constantly renews her spell
this thread protects me from all strife.
It brought me back from where I ran
with crazy notions in my head
this sorry creature that I am
I couldn't live without my thread
but thoughts like these will see me through
because my golden thread is you.

An angel surely let me know...

For I would walk my love, with you
down lanes and through these pastures green
and we would talk as good friends do
of joy and life, in mood serene.
For man could find no better mate
than life-long's lover by his side
with things as these to cogitate
and stroll along in time's great tide.
And as we glide along in peace
we talk and laugh enjoying life
my love continually doth increase
for you the one who is my wife.
To have found you so long ago
and loved you then as I do now
an angel surely let me know
the route to your heart, and the how.
If other men had love as mine
to grow and last a lifetime through
had lives all filled with hearts divine
and days of joy and romance new.
Such joy they too would countenance
and lives that feel so much more fine
as they cavort through merry dance
in life so wondrous such as mine.

To Express Oneself...

Were I a man less fortunate
If I could not my words express
Would I not humbly shun the light
And all my boundless thoughts compress.
My heart is full and begs release
Outpourings flow from deep within
And words flood out and take their form
Of love and pain, and life and sin.
To sit and wait these countless times
Considering this or that to say
Thoughts writ in beguiling form
Thus written they then speed on their way.
Characters flit betwixt mine eyes
So fast sometimes I cannot catch
Letters caught in mêlée furious
I place them here or there to match.
When all these letters are thus laid down
In words to make some form or sense
Then read by one's discerning eye
With open mind and no pretense.
Who reads these words I cannot know
But surely if when read they think
That thoughts they have become theirs now
Thus quill or pen make seamless link.

My many coloured life...

Colour me brown for the woods I played in as a boy
For the bow and arrows I used for a toy
For the friends and the fun and the unfettered joy.
Colour me beige for my calm and neutral look at life
The nothingness that could have been spread with a knife
The colour I felt before I loved my wife.
Colour me green for the nature that surrounds
For the children we had and their ever happy sounds
For the promise that their future hopes abound.
Colour me cream for your quiet elegant ways
That fill my life with beautiful days
The joy of being in a life-long phase.
Colour me blue for the truth you speak
For the trust you gave when my life was bleak
For the quiet solitude we sometimes seek.
Colour me pink for the true love you give
For the beauty of each and every day that we live
For the small thoughtless sins that you always forgive.
Colour me red for the passion we still feel
For each other a passion that is still very real
For the hearts that we tied with an emotional seal.
Colour me purple for the compassion you hold
For the sensitive spirits that with you unfold
For the judgement and dreams that help me feel bold.
Colour me yellow for the wisdom you set free
For the knowledge I learnt so empowering to see
For the sunshine in your heart saved especially for me.
Colour me all these colours magnificently
You gave to me a life far less ordinary
You gave me your love and you showed to me...me.

SYMPHONY OF SOULS

❧

Richard J. Panizza

❧

"Blow Out"

As when
all seems to be going well
There is
suddenly a blow out that throws
You off the
trident beaten path

Thrown
into a ditch with a flatten tire

Nothing
ever expected
Certainly
never desired

Caught in a
sudden crisis pulling for the
Spare

The
recourse being the tire iron to where
There's no
grip to be sufficient for any do

Replacement

The only
resolve is to walk the many miles
Back to the
homeward bound

Deep with
in the night the distance is now
Double

SYMPHONY OF SOULS

fold

Eventually
destination is discovered
At least
that's the solace told

Finally the
arrival of safety peace is
Found

Now relief
is the destined point of sanctity
In psyche
to then be bound

"Dreams Come and Go"

The very essence of your heart
Your soul being your reasoning
For continuing –
Striving on ward for, from the very
Start

From when you had begun
To where you end up being

Some do come true
While others tragically fail relegated
To the ash heaps of your life's history
Never again to then be seen.

Either way
Regardless of success or failure alike
Never do cease dreaming

Keep the spirit alive
Keep moving to survive

Always hold on to what is more than a
Feeling but, rather is the very means to
That all remains and much more pertinently,
Strives

"The Photographer"

The photographer
forever remains still behind
The camera's lens

Forever capturing the
eternal memories in the
Light prisms that never
end

The very essence of our
soul's remembrance
Of days now past

Days of our promised
dreams

Some fulfilled of lives
requited
Others discovered lying
in ruins shattered

All though rendered in
our time's eternity

The records that shall
ever last

But, who are they
The ones whom of
which forever remain dutifully
Still behind the frame

The individual that
captures our life's records

SYMPHONY OF SOULS

Standing alone with not
the shared memories of
The lighted replicated
recorded fortunes or even
Fame

It is, indeed, the
photographer whom of which is
Responsible for
capturing our soul's in times
Eternity retained intact
forever complete, as well as,
Whole

"Mutual Ground"

Perhaps I should ad-lib this
song
The same as you took us
for granted

Only to discover that we,
indeed,
Were strong

To find that you were
definitely wrong

I gave you the very best of
what I could

Christ's sakes I worked for
our romance
Undying

But, obviously I didn't work
as hard as
I have should

Now our love lies wasted upon
the broken
Vine

The resources of our love have
now ran thin

Free frustration is now forever
on its edge
Tipping downward and falling
over end

SYMPHONY OF SOULS

Never, ever to begin again

I realize that you are not either to
blame

Perhaps we have to reserve our
sanity and
Call it the end

It is the grief repeated I now know
shall
Never, ever really mend

Time goes by to leave us behind

The days now pass fast to see
history be blind

If only we knew that our passion
could turn to
Hatred and pain

We then could stop the romance from
the
Repeated, endless refrain

Every time the jury is out and
sequestered
They announce the unbiased verdict

Innocent I seem to be found

Now tell me why our affair could never
rest upon any
Mutual ground

"I Awaken Dazed"
-(In the Middle of the Night)-

There's a thunder clap that rings loud in
My ear

I awaken dazed in the middle of the night

Disturbed by the endless nightmare and a
Cold intrepid fear

Oh, my God ever since I lost you, I had
Never known such a fright

Do you feel the same that I do

Maybe if we would try it again we would
Make it through

We both know that would be living a
Damned lie

The fact of matter is that our love leads
Only to tears pouring like rain from cold
Darkened skies

But, still remember the time when we held
Each other so very dear

We thought our love would last forever with
No contention or fear

Fear of a viseral split to where we would
Both be left only in our love's shattered tears

SYMPHONY OF SOULS

I try to fight back all the tears

I wake up in the middle of the evening calling
Your name

Your absence sends a chill through my soul I
Could have never imagined

You or I, the tragic fate of our love is that
We're both to blame

SYMPHONY OF SOULS

Antonio Duarte

Fool to believe?

Am I a fool to believe?
To think that there might be
For me, a place in your life?

The thought of want
Has me scaling my walls
Climb your minaret
Immerse myself
'Neath the skin
Just so that I can become a part of you
Even if it's harder and hurts more

My faith is all I've got
Seems to think otherwise
For this fool has come to believe
That you have cast a spell upon my soul

Descendant of shadows
I've returned back into
Awaiting your beckoning
From among a flock of iridescence's caw

Am I a fool to believe?
Waiting for the sun
To hang himself out to dry
And sink into dusk fading light
Bring on the still of night
Like death that approaches with his dense coldness
You can see my hot breath in the frigid air

Soul shivering
Bones quivering
Marrow solidifying

SYMPHONY OF SOULS

Waiting for you to touch the moon with your eyes
So that I will be able to catch you from upon mine
Hanging on to the fringes of your ghost

Am I a fool to believe?

Never Ending Journey

Where to go from here?

How to get to where I wanna be
From where I'm at?

It's a continuous long journey thus far
Every day of my life
It begins as soon as I open these eyes
At this moment it feels as if I've come to an end somehow
My life has temporarily stopped
Yet time keeps dragging on

Contemplating...

I begin to drift apart from self
Fading further away from life

Being separated from clay sheet
Traveling backwards at light speed
Reverting back to my childhood

I'm sitting in the car
My dad is driving down S.W Military Dr.
And I'm staring all at life
Passing right before my eyes
Noticing all these roads
Along the byways and highways
Perplexed as to where do they lead to and where they end

I use believe that all these roads in life led to one road
Taking me on out where it meets the beach and staring into
and ocean view

Is this the end?.......................................

SYMPHONY OF SOULS

I asked my dad, " Dad, do these roads end?"

His reply was, " for some they do Son, others they keep going on for miles. But the road itself never ends, only for the ones who journey it."

(I don't know why I'm crying while I'm writing this. Large tears run down off my eyes and river down my cheeks into my beard. Oh how I miss you so Dad)

And just like that
I come back
My pops journey upon his road has ended
As his soul awaits like a stone
Patiently in a room all alone

And I asked myself

Where to go from here?

How to get to where I wanna be
From where I'm at?

My road has not yet ended
Just an end to this page
From upon my journals that this poetic heart in which I write,
baring my soul
For I'm bout to embark into a new chapter in life
I shall see what the new year brings
For I have many miles to feet
Before my soul becomes a stone

(Crying hard again)
Thank you pops for coming to me
Revealing my revelation

SYMPHONY OF SOULS

Witnessing a flock of ravens
Ascending back into which they came from
My dads spirit rises from their eyes
Back into the gig in the sky..

Set sail

Set my sails
Heart set on no direction in mind
Just go with the breeze
In where ever it may lead me
Although my soul's compass needle
Inching due south, Bowling Green
So now I'm on my way to the falcon city
For some odd reason
I'm being petitioned

Audio slave's putrid
Spilling out raw sewage
Thru my speakers
While staring into the unknown
Of a predestined journey
That have already been in-scripted
Awaiting me, like acts
Upon the stage, like onion pages
Myriads from among the ceiling
Witnessing the instance of me setting out from my exodus

Sailing across the asphalt sea
Allow Helios to shine his beams into these darken eyes
And there I am singin along
One with my spirit
Shadow of the sun
With ominous of iridescence within my vie
Below my comraderer, the sky

For some reason
Im feelin uneasy
But I don't care
Cause I can't see what behind the veil
That's in front of me

SYMPHONY OF SOULS

Didn't realize without thinking
I was headed straight for you
Like a beacon, lost out at sea
I'm the highway begins its psalm
finally I arrive, with no intentions at all
Where the river flows and the old rail yard
Track thirteen begins to hymn
I'm a slave for his audio
Chris Cornell, personal Jesus walks upon the water of my
being

Pullin in
Passin Isaac Lugwig Mill
Thru the bridge of sighs
And there,   it all makes perfect sense
Finally realizing
But too late to do anything
But allow it to unravel
Catching you in my sights
Like a deer to headlights
Walking down the old historic town
Creme de la creme, feminine abyss
Soul sings our getaway car by then
Staring into the truth till I'm blind
Its been months since I've seen you
I can see the whites in your wide eyes
As you heave a deep heavy breath
Ha, the emotion is mutual
And like slow motion we locked eyes
You, walking on, me, driving by

Didn't know it at the time
Waves would be sailing me this way
Fate up against our will
What are the odds
Destiny brought us together

SYMPHONY OF SOULS

Synchronizing our skies to align with perfect time
To catch your soul upon mine

I'm not gonna lie
It was good to see you
And for a moment in time
Everything stopped
Hearts skip beats
I can feel yours within mine
Even if I could, I would never stop the dance
Floating out of this town upon the eternity of my love that will
always burn deep in my soul for you

Strange how life puts us on paths unknown

All of a sudden life speeds up
I'm awaken by honks
Catching the last remnants of you
From out of the corners of my peripherals
Quickly a fix my gaze and watched you fade from my rear
view and trying to keep from crashing into oncoming traffic

Tears begin to rain heavy
Falling, hitting my chest like bullets
I start to die
Heart aches with pain
Burns with hurt
Soul weeps like a willow
Yearns for your return

Replay Getaway car

And with this I start to die
Soul sheds from mortal vessel
No fear, paying the price
Ashes to ashes
Black waves from the asphalt sea

SYMPHONY OF SOULS

Starts to crash
Louder and louder
My love starts to cry
Seeing you standing there
Watching me leave
As I watch you fade away
I've reached my threshold

I'm your getaway car

All that I need

All that I want with you, is a new moon
All that I'll ever need is a new moon

New moon, new moon
New moon, new moon

Waxing and waning

All that I am, is all I'm ever gonna be
All that I am, is all I'm ever gonna be

So here I am
Take what you need
Here I am
I'm all that you see

New moon, new moon
New moon, new moon

All I'm ever gonna ask
All I'm ever gonna ask
Is for your skies to be above my earth
Soles walking upon me
Breathing your air, inhaling
Footprints embedded into my soul

For all I'm ever gonna be
I'm gonna be in your stare
And when its time for you to go
I'll be upon horizon watching you leaving, like dusk fading
sun

You'll be taking with you
In what you have already stole from me
My heart in that which is intended, my beautiful thief

You're the air I breathe
I'm the earth you need
Sweeping your silent breeze all thru me
I can hear you, I can hear you, I can hear you

All that I want with you, is a new moon
All that I'll ever need is a new moon

New moon, new moon
New moon, new moon

Waxing and waning

Broken Home

Ain't nothing like coming into what's already been broken
No matter how much you mend it
The amount of glue will never adhere
To what was once was

Never will it be the same

Bunch of broken pieces put together
From upon a dysfunctional family
A kitchen that already has no soul

Sittin all alone
Microwave on
Counting the minutes
For my cup-o-soup to be done
Its is all you'll find

My dads playing X-box and throwin the nerf
My eleven year looks at me

"Whats wrong Dad?"

"Nothing daddy"

"Why you look so depressed? "

"It's nothing, man"

Leans in for a hug
Tears shed

"Take your medicine dad, chuck up them tears"

SYMPHONY OF SOULS

A final hug
With a confession of "I love you dad"

"Love you (tears) too,daddy

Romeo Della Valle

Allusion

There is a contradiction
In wanting to be understood
And finding no explanation
Worthy of the question!

Allusion is not evasion
But a hint to discovery
Revealing broader perception
Than stiff definition!

A Weary Poet

Buried in blue and yellow,
Beneath fire blankets
And a bold maroon comforter,
One sheet lumped in a corner,
I am just warm enough
To be unselfishly conscious
Even of my own thoughts!

Absent of physical strain,
Tired, I try to focus
While holding my magic pen,
Which carries a precious secret?
But it floats away
Like music once it passed
The secret way
While going out preserved,
Totally undisturbed!

Suddenly, I heard a loud voice
This seemed to remove the distance,
Perhaps, it was my soul,
Speaking to me of worthy things
Or urging my heart to be willing!

Now, I am seeking more
Than hiding behind my weariness,
Looking into the darkest bright,
Seeing riddles hidden in my soul
And questioning at the same time
My broken and stubborn heart,

Why do you still refuse
To reconcile with my eased mind?
No answer precipitates the air
Breathing this weary poet!

Majestic Rain

Feeling beating down
Like rain above rooftops,
Little droplets splashing
Against black and surfaces
Of shingled dwellings!

Gracefully falling
With forceful steadiness,
heaven's tears sent to Earth,
Condensed into volumes
Of eternity!

Wandering minstrels
Of immortality
Roam the skies before
With more sentiment!

A Creative Mind

The solid foundation of an ideal
Is the equivalent to the depth
Of the mind and the hands
Which design destiny!

Borders outlined
By the possibility of success
Delineating the horizons
Of a renew energy of life!

Entirely new,
Outer dimensions,
Dissolve the staleness,
Replacing it with creativity!

Cosmic and dynamic forces
Are all counterparts
Of a unique shaped form
Which has no end or beginning
Like a circumference!

Poignant and rich thoughts
Freely traversing the universe
And breaking the barrier of time
To carry the true message of:
"Love and Peace for always"!

LIKE A BRANDED NOTE

Selflessness is best
But insanity is contagious,
Where friendship disembarks
A whole ship of fools!

Better to jump overboard
Than to cast your lot
Among those
whom evil has caught
In a dirty pool!

My bay be solitude
Cast off without fortitude,
The night remains my harbor friend
Where daytime ceases not to pain!

Wings without feathers cease to flap-
Lacking impetus- they waxen flat,
A conscience inside a bottle afloat
And my life rolled up
Like a branded note!

༄

Jahanshah Rashidian

༄

' I Float Away '

I Float Away
More alive, than death buries me
Less vanquished than victory elates
My ardor is brighter than a torch
A soul immune to vigilance
Well safe through my soul
I float away, where the nature has promised.

Heavier under the scepter of the devil
Less burdensome than the suspicion of rumor
Mature enough to convince me only nothingness
Well released from my daytime chimera
I float away, where my other self waits.

More ardent hung on my sources
Less wrapped in my dying flesh
Enough spent my carnal body
Well held the cosmos to its tail
I float away to the nature's desire.

' Under your Scarf '

Under your scarf covering your hair
As if you were hiding
A sapphire treasure
At the bottom of the ocean
Whose raven jets sparkle.

Under your black scarf
As if you were hiding
Caresses repressed
In your hair growing thirsty
In the darkest destiny.

Under your sacred scarf
As if you were hiding
Your profane hair
For the wanton sin
That no one forgives.

Under your thick scarf
As if you were hiding
Your braids listless
Like lackluster seaweed
Beneath the ocean
Abandoning light.

Under your prudently toned scarf
As if you were hiding
The burdening sin
Of every gaze of a man
That his sensuality feels.

Under your confidential scarf
Your hair unveils

SYMPHONY OF SOULS

The loops that you hide
But that weave your destiny
With the eclipse of your star in the East..

' *Echo* '

Echoes of history in my ears fill time-lapses
The screaming chimes of ringing collapses
Forgotten crimes of dark apocalypses
I can see all when time elapses.

Echoes in time will lose resonance
If love were a lonely performance
Bloodshed would lose common sense
The bloody earth would hold no substance.

Infidel bloodshed is not their remorse
With shine of sword within their eyes
They are divinely morose
So our happy minds amazingly froze.

They painted our horizon with shadows
With dim lines snaking through meadows
Their victims as marionettes of fore-shows
Float between the chord and gallows.

All these times through shadows of darkness
Light and freedom had no access
As they broke our pens of awareness
Their dark scripts still tighten our shackles.

' Eternal Love '

Love is my envy to be by her side
not like a butterfly's fancy
before his death
flailing moments around the candle.
The butterfly resumes love in the candle
The candle burns his wings.

But, in my remote horizon
I gallop towards the eternal love
with rhymes of my heart
as a ballad in my horse's hooves.

What will be love?
When with my horse's stirrups
another ode wishes it a long life
more than a lovelorn butterfly
around his beloved candle.

' *Migrant Sparrow* '

Each morning
With a migrant sparrow skipping around
In the light of the window frame
I wake up from sleep.

Urges hidden in her wings
Up to me through half-closed eyes
To spray mist of light
That is sprinkled with shades of night
On the ceiling of my room.

As if during the incident
For a moment the roof filters
Particles of light and life
From four arches of crumbling sky.

At these quiet moments, the sparrow
Waits for the night from my bed.

Inevitably night is over
And the sparrow
With the shadows of the night
Flies away.

༄

Fátima Coutinho

༄

' Never the pleasure of seeing my face '

Sitting in a marvelous cafe
with splendid of Brazilian music
The candlelight on the table
illuminates truths
from the depths of my soul
I am dreaming as always
nothing strange
friends call me a princess
of soulful dreams
My path is of a lonely hermit
dark, without any hues
despite sunshine
displaying a philharmonic show
of a ballet dancing on a scene

How many times I return to my chapel
the one where I am meeting God
I pray for hours and ... God is listening
He is calm and attentive
helping me to understand
all the things I don't
that are happening around me
and in the world itself

Inside this silent retreat
in the chapel of God
I am trying my best
to hear and understand
every single Word of His
This world is so camouflaged!
But when I walk out of my chapel
I feel born again

SYMPHONY OF SOULS

Perhaps there is a chance
I can be happy again

But then reality is back
my nightmares take over me
I no longer know
whether I am alive or dead
There were amazing things
happening centuries before Christ
A window said to the ceiling
- ' You will never have the pleasure
of seeing my face! '
And the ceiling refuted, mocking
- ' Since when does window have a face? '

I returned the same way, amid people
surrounded by towering groves
A trail that leads back to me
and embellishes adventures revived by me
In the constant traveling
which I do with my creative mind
and in my inner soulful worlds

' Bleak '

Ghosts appear and vanish
while the flames of a candle
dance by my bed
Every time the wind blows
into my bedroom through the open window
I don't know whether I sleep
I think I'd rather lay awake

I drift alone in my kingdom
The cock crows, it is already dawn
but I am still asleep, dreaming
The rays of the sun wake me
And I see wonder upon wonders
flowers in the garden, their serene softness
displaying their wondrous grace

My world is hopelessly dark
as if there are no windows
in my beautiful house
I look at the wonders outside the windows
at the flowers dancing their waltz
Catwalk colors through the glass
show a model beauty
it's me, fascinating all onlookers

Wreath of flowers, my arms ensnare
Passion burns in my chest
Alone in the dark of my nightmares
that didn't pass in the night
gone in tears, unhappy, crying
why these nightmares, why loneliness?
How can I free myself from the demons' snare!
Say it, please say!

SYMPHONY OF SOULS

I want to enjoy the beauty of the morning
and forget everything that is bad
No longer confined to my fears
engulfing me in all those dreams

'Avenue '

I walked that avenue yesterday
and will remember it
until my last breath
I despaired. I cried
and didn't want
to accept that mirage
Walking alone, unknown
among passersby, forgotten
a lonely woman in red

My world arched on that avenue
my dream arched there too
My eyes wept from your departure
You were my angel, the perfect dream
which disappeared with you

The memory of you
is now a nightmare for me
I wake up in the middle of the night
and silently scream
' Who's face is this?
Whose eyes are these? '
Wake up and make another dream!
Find hope in your soul

And you, my dear lover from my dreams
See you soon
in the next avenue

' *Passage* '

I am the cry of the wind without echo
I am the fruit of sin Adam condemned
I am the pearl on the Pacific floor
I came from the bottom of valleys
where no foot stepped before

Go to the clearest lake
the kingdom of the moon
I am the wild wind
singing beautiful songs to our souls
I am the essence of life, the fear of death
Run through the darkness
without leaving any traces

Spending eternity with my beloved
without him noticing
my longing to place
Condemning me to life
which inspires me to death

While autumn seems to nurture me
no one notices when you come and go
While dwelling in this land
I will perform all my duties
I do not even know
if I do this for love or obligation

You see I am a believer
The Bible says
everything has been given
as a punishment
I no longer know

SYMPHONY OF SOULS

whether I hate or love
this biblical punishment

I am everything and I am nothing
I am the fog in the winter
I am the heat in summer
I come and go as autumn
I was born in the darkness, yet
I live to the fullness of the sunshine
so long as life dwells in me

' I'll walk, I'll run '
/ Without time and age /

Poetry is without time or age
A high mountain not knowing
what is insecurity and fear
Poetry is beauty and grace
our Earthly paradise song
a paradise of birds
staying together, flying together, singing together

I'll walk, I'll run, I'll fight back
You better flee to the land of Saturn
I do not want your influence on me
And know it my path is clear
and your fall one day
shall become a dream come true
The sun will come and utopia with it!

Perhaps I want what I can't have
but it's still not the end of the world
because I am in a fighting spirit
and I shall show what I can!
I am like a skyrocketing eagle
there is nothing I can't!

I look in the mirror and see myself
like a flower of a paradise
among angels playing on harps
Those around me in this Earthly life
cannot see me as I really am
They think I am sad
they think I despair, even mourn
How mistaken they are

SYMPHONY OF SOULS

'cause I am a joy of all joys!

Perhaps there is a chance
someone though will hear me
Those who will hear me
will enjoy eternal destiny
and who will not, well, it's not my problem
My feet goes bare, the sand off the trail
I follow the steps
and do not know where they will end
In hell or in heaven?
Or in the cosmic shell of my own ego?
Well, I should know it better
and trust the Lord!

But I am not alone, I'm me
combating the wicked
and toasting a victory
In the clouds which hide my dreams
there is still a chance for you and me
Come, my prince of my dreams
I want to be your princess
and you won't be disappointed, believe me
There was a lame horse
abandoned on the road
to apotheosis
but I am still here, for you

I know it's your trick, my prince
High Mountain, insecurity and fear
will be left far behind
I shall be a princess in a castle
on the horizons of your heart, my prince

People will sing songs
about the sad, young woman
who found refuge in you, my prince

SYMPHONY OF SOULS

and sweet poems
limitless of time and age
will be an unstoppable trend

We shall be united
and stay together
without time and age
Joy will be our life
for all times to come

꙰

Ken Blick

꙰

All Men Do

Sometimes when I say,
the things that I do.
They are probably lies,
none of it true.
I did what I did,
so I could have you.
I say things to get in your head,
just so I can get you in bed.
There's nothing that I won't say,
Its a man thing, we do it everyday.
Women fall for it each and every time,
and their convinced this should be a Federal crime.
Listen to what I'm telling you,
this is something that all men do.
I hope you don't hate me for saying that,
I'm only point out the truth and a Man fact.
I'm not meaning you no ill will,
Yet I know your gonna fall for it still.
So don't come shedding your tears back to me,
I did my best to warn you but you girls never see.
I gotta go now and it's been really fun,
I have to move on because our time here is done.
I hope you don't start to cry,
I just wanted to tell you so you learn next time.
It's a Man thing
and that's our reason why.

SYMPHONY OF SOULS

It's True

The Lord sent you to me,

I know that's true.

I wanna spend the rest of my life,

Loving you.

What can I do?

I'm crazy 'bout you.

.

I remember just before we met,

I had it all, I was set.

And then you came through the door,

telling me there was much more.

I surrendered as you told me to,

like you said, Jesus would do.

.

I stepped out of myself

and into the light.

SYMPHONY OF SOULS

I gave up everything that night,

for you,

and Jesus too.

.

You saved me,

now can I save you?

I see that your heart is blue.

What can I do?

I'm so crazy 'bout you.

.

Love never lived in my heart,

until you came along I was stark.

Over time I knew it was you.

I'm praising God,

because I know it's true.

I'm in love with you.

.

SYMPHONY OF SOULS

Take my hand and believe in me,

I'm not the man you once seen.

You raised me up when I was down,

never gave up,

and I won't now.

That's true,

because I'm crazy 'bout you.

Will you love me too?

SYMPHONY OF SOULS

The Revival

I gave my heart to Jesus, many years ago.

It was at a revival, toward the end of the show.

A man came up and said, "Brother just come on in,

and let the blood of Jesus, just wash away that sin."

When I walked on in,

I could see it happening.

People were dancing and raising their arms in the air.

(LIKE THEY JUST DIDN'T CARE!!)

[Chorus]

They were shouting "Praise the lord!"

(PRAISE THE LORD)

They were swinging to and fro!

(PRAISE THE LORD)

They were laughing and singing

and simply praising the lord!

SYMPHONY OF SOULS

(PRAISE THE LORD)

Hallelujah thank you Christ,

Heaven will be so nice,

now that you know my name.

I will live like I believe.

I won't cower or deceive,

and my life will never be the same.

(PRAISE THE LORD)

My head began to spin.

I didn't know what was happening.

Next thing I knew,

that man was back again.

(HE SAID)

"My name is Father Dunn,

and I've been where your coming from.

Just take a seat,

because we've only just begun."

(HE SAID)

SYMPHONY OF SOULS

"The Lord won't be beat,

so stop beating up yourself.

Your only a sinner,

but you can be so much else.

Stop trying to be something your not.

Your wearing yourself out,

trying to keep ahead of the lot.

Just slow on down and let Jesus in,

surrender your worries,

and start living again."

[Chorus]

So, I gave my heart to Jesus at that revival show.

I made up my mind to fight no more.

I started to say hello and I started to care some more.

Before I knew it,

Jesus had my soul!!

(PRAISE THE LORD)

SYMPHONY OF SOULS

Thy Eternal

When I said goodnight, you said goodbye.

Our last kiss was in the night.

I drifted off to sleep,

and the lord took your soul to keep.

The sun no longer rises in the East.

I wallow like a rabid beast.

When God took you away from me,

he chained my heart, I can't break free.

Take my riches, take my fame,

even sully my good name.

Give to me just one more chance,

one more night and one last dance.

I'm feeling low and feeling blue,

in life it was always me and you.

I know I can never be free,

when you died you took the key.

SYMPHONY OF SOULS

****

Dearest love,

I am here,

beyond your sight,

but still so near.

I watch you as you go to sleep.

I am there when you start to weep.

I am beside you everyday.

I am there when you kneel and pray.

I will be here when you pass,

and welcome you home

when it's your time at last.

TIME

Time.
I'm sure it was passing,
but inside our bubble,
it did not exist.
Neither did people,
although they were all around us.
We were not alone,
yet at the same time,
we were.
Everything was silent
except for your voice
and the beating of my heart.
My ears were like hot coals
sitting upon a cast iron pot.
It was winter
but you had me in a sweat.
I still don't understand
how my mumblings made you smile.
The touch of your hand upon my arm
sent shivers through me.
When I looked into those eyes,
I was amazed to see your soul.
Time.
We were lost in
Time.

Elluisa Granath - Vargas Conroy

Heaven's Gate

As I sit here with deep thoughts
How I'm full of so much rage
Must I truly keep it locked up
Deep inside or release from my cage?
This pain she has caused
Runs through so deep
I lay here at night tossing, turning,
All I can do is sit and stew
But mostly weep.
A mothers love is supposed to
Be unconditional with no terms
I try my hardest to shine like a star
She continues to tell me to burn.
I must continue to be me
To fight remain strong
No matter what comes my way
I must carry on.
Even though this truly, deeply
Kills me inside
I act as if nothing bothers me
Just another day die or ride.
I choose to ride with
No looking back what's done
Is done she chose to leave,
I'm not one to run.
So take your hate,
Your gossip. And discriminate
I know where I'm going I hope
To see you at Heavens Gate.

I'm Alive

My pulse drops to 29
I'm doing everything to hold on.
Staying focused,
Staying strong.
Knowing its not my time.
I still have work to be done
Can't say a word but blink my eyes
To let everyone know
I'm still with them,
I'm not in the skies,
And I'm alive.
All I can think about
Is I have kids to raise.
In my spirit I'm on my knees
For its you God that I praise.
Please don't take me.
My kids need me
I'm all they have.
My children are only 8 and 3.
Please Lord don't let this be my time.
So here I am now
With a story to tell.
If you're a believer
And know God
God delivered and healed me.
Its true that He spared my life
To do His work.
I'm here to spread the love of Jesus.
I was dying of kidney failure.

SYMPHONY OF SOULS

My liver functions were starting to go.
Then I was about
To have a pacemaker in my heart.
Now I have none.
The Lord gave me life
And a new start.
So now its time for me
To do my part.

A Mother's Love

A mother holds you
close to her heart
trying so hard
to do her part.

Teaching you
how to be, before she is too old
treasuring you and treating you
like gold.

A mothers work
is truly never done
life seems so crazy
always on the run.

So gentle and true
going through the motion
giving baths and rubbing
you down with lotion.

Time at a glance
without a moment to pass
as if you were watching
through a looking glass.

A mothers love
never dies
she is always there
willing to give you another try.

How To say Goodbye

I see it is your time to go home
You have left us behind
With all these feeling of love
Hurt and emotions that start to roam

Why you had to leave we will never know
This rips our hearts as the tears that pour
The loneliness overwhelms
Please just remember we love you so.

Sad how our lives can change in a blink of an eye
When do we know it is okay to let go?
Will we ever feel safe again? Is it okay to love?
How do you know when it is time to say good bye?

Letting go of a loved one is so hard
When is it right?
How do you know?
Does it just come to you like throwing ball in a yard?

Time must go on
The emotions are strong
But there is nothing left
My daddy is gone.

Silence

As I sit here no sound
With dreams of being bound
Tied in confusion
With no one around.
No one in sight
I cant even find a light
How can this be the end of ones night?
Sense of being alone with no one to speak
Every where I go I hear them whisper of me
As some kind of freak.
Being different then others
locking myself inside
Don't want to be sad
Always trying to hide.
Grabbing this feeling
I have stuffed so deep within
Like caring a
Huge bag of sin.
Here I lay in silence
All these taunted thoughts
Needing to let them out
Praying to God to please end all this violence
As I scream and shout.

∂

Thaddeus Hutyra

∂

' *Fires of Phoenix* '

Once upon a time
love story is burning
in our hearts
like the fires of Phoenix
stormy waterfalls of our feelings
skyline rivers of clouds

There is a secret home
inside our souls turned one soul
where our lives
are projected
in all dimensions

A magic film
showing us both
on fierce fire of love
as we were
when we loved each other

A tragic one
when you said ' Good bye '
and I have never seen you again
But though you're gone
I can watch you over and over

A would be one
showing us both
if we had never separated
living together
in our oasis of love

Say, say, why have you gone
my babe

SYMPHONY OF SOULS

Say, say, what was wrong with us
that you had decided
to leave me

I have gone this time away
to the Far East
trying to forget you
China girls are smiling
tempting … promising …

Yet I know it now
I won't ever forget you
Love is amaranthine
a temple in our soul
a starship across Universe

No twists of life
shall end my love
no distracted starry rays
no shortcoming memory
neither the passing time

I firmly believe
we shall meet one day
A triumph of love, our love
will pierce through nightly skies
and deep inside our soul, our home

SYMPHONY OF SOULS

' Symphony of Angels '

Angel on the pathways of stars
playing music with his harp
He is emanating
with his male beauty
all the female angels are in love!

Angel on the pathways of stars
is playing the music of the stars
on his beloved amaranthine harp
Inspired
his dreams flowing
to the tunes of his heartbeat
his mind filled with overwhelming love
his soul dancing among the stars

Angel on the pathways of stars
he, the master of virtuosity
His harp extension of him himself
celestial sounds beam into the stars
and far beyond
They reach the Earth

Angel on the pathways of stars
overwhelmed by his love
his Hamlet alike dilemma
Well, why not love

SYMPHONY OF SOULS

what's wrong with love?!

He plays his harp in divine ways
the sounds reaching the stars
whatever problems they are forgotten
music is the king and queen
the music which multiplies the stars

Do you hear it, my dear reader
who isn't in this masterful play?!
Puccini and Verdi, Mozart and Debussy
Vittorio Monti, Andre Caplet, Paganini
Oh, dance and sing, God's angels!

What a metamorphosis happens then
it's not just our beloved angel
but plenty of female angels around him
with unimaginable beauty
adoring him, loving him
joining him in a symphonic play
one uniting the paradise and Earth

What happens next
is larger than life, far beyond
quintessential of the worlds
between human and celestial
the symphony of angels
playing both for the Heavens and Earth

SYMPHONY OF SOULS

' *America, America* '

America, America
God's Garden of Eden
cherishing freedoms
as shown in the first ten amendments
of American constitution
called collectively the Bill of Rights

America, America
land of the Founding Fathers
George Washington, Benjamin Franklin
Thomas Jefferson, John Adams ...
Land of great men gone too soon
Abraham Lincoln, Martin Luther King

America, America
an example of heroic country
at peace and war
Land of dramas
as those of the Kennedy tragedies
commonly known as the Kennedy curse

America, America
wounded America
in the nine eleventh
Although WTC twin towers are gone
the Freedom Tower
stands there triumphantly

America, America
the flower of humanity
rising high into the starry skies
Land of the Space Shuttle
Enterprise, Columbia, Challenger,
Discovery, Atlantis, Endeavor

SYMPHONY OF SOULS

America, America
soul of a great nation
of people from all corners of the world
dynamic
still searching
and rising like an immortal Phoenix

America, America
don't let your heart and soul
be poisoned by those
who wish you bad luck
Show the mankind
the right path towards the stars

' *Rendezvous* '

How many times
we had our rendezvous
in our heart, our home
No finest villa, greatest place
could ever match it

You knocked to my heart
entered, threw your hands
around my neck
and was hanging so
for long, joyful time

Then we kissed
and starry skies
began to shine
to the tunes of our hearts
turned one heart, of love

Although our home
stayed high on the cliffs
of San Francisco Bay
we were not afraid
Love was the queen

Our heart, our home
was like thousands of iPhones
singing melodies of love
I love you, I love you
skyrocketed beyond the stars

And yet we stayed
entwined in our arms
within our heart, our home
promising to each other

SYMPHONY OF SOULS

we shall stay together forever

'cause our love was greater than life
one of Romeo and Juliet
We wanted to turn our fate around
make our love
a permanent feature

Sitting on the cliffs
of San Francisco Bay
we know now
we have succeeded
Our heart, our home
stays on and shall stay

' *My Lord* '

He was kneeling on the forest clearing
under the moonless, unwelcoming sky
decorated though by the pearly stars
My Lord, he prayed, with tears in his eyes
bring me away from my dire misery
change my fate, change my destiny, please

Oh, ring, ring, ring in my soul, my Lord
tinkle, tinkle, tinkle in my heart, my Lord
buzz, buzz, buzz in my ears, my Lord
jingle, jingle, jingle in my head, my Lord
thunder, thunder in my mind, my Lord
let me be loved, forever loved, my Lord

I loved her more than anything else
she was my singing bluebird, my angel
my dear treasure, dearest in the world
Yet she is gone now for good, for no reason
and no chance to see her again, I fear
My Lord, bring her back to me, please

Oh, ring, ring, ring in my soul, my Lord
tinkle, tinkle, tinkle in my heart, my Lord
buzz, buzz, buzz in my ears, my Lord
jingle, jingle, jingle in my head, my Lord
rumble and resound, and echo, my Lord

SYMPHONY OF SOULS

let me be loved, forever loved, my Lord

The sky seemed to be a symphony of souls
in which the brightly effervescent stars
were like plentiful of celestial, starry pianos
their keyboards touched by God's Hand
The three tenors seemed to be heard
alongside the starry philharmonic play

Oh, ring, ring, ring in my soul, my Lord
tinkle, tinkle, tinkle in my heart, my Lord
buzz, buzz, buzz in my ears, my Lord
jingle, jingle, jingle in my head, my Lord
ignite sparks of change in my fate, my Lord
let me be loved, forever loved, my Lord

He was still kneeling on the forest clearing
praying the whole night, weeping at times
He could never ever agree with his loss
by no longer having her at his side
no longer hearing her crystal voice
her laugh of pure joy, seeing her happy face

Oh, ring, ring, ring in my soul, my Lord
tinkle, tinkle, tinkle in my heart, my Lord
buzz, buzz, buzz in my ears, my Lord
jingle, jingle, jingle in my head, my Lord
thunder, thunder with lightnings, my Lord
let me be loved, forever loved, my Lord

SYMPHONY OF SOULS

At the twilighted dawn, with plenty of hues
when the stars were slowly disappearing
and the celestial philharmonic play
was accentuated by evolving rays of the Sun
piercing through the shield of the dawn
he stood up and headed home, though unhappy

Oh, ring, ring, ring in my soul, my Lord
tinkle, tinkle, tinkle in my heart, my Lord
buzz, buzz, buzz in my ears, my Lord
jingle, jingle, jingle in my head, my Lord
resound with your good will, my Lord
let me be loved, forever loved, my Lord

What was his delightful surprise when he saw
the woman he loved the most stood there
on the doorstep, with welcoming hands
He ran to her and took her in his arms
made a whirlwind dance, then kissed her
God heard him, she was back with him !

Oh, ring, ring, ring in my soul, my Lord
tinkle, tinkle, tinkle in my heart, my Lord
buzz, buzz, buzz in my ears, my Lord
jingle, jingle, jingle in my head, my Lord
reverberate with good news, my Lord
be thanked, forever thanked, my Lord

SYMPHONY OF SOULS

The Authors/Poets of this fabulous Anthology would like to thank you the readers for your constant love and support.

"May these words bring a melody to your hearts and a Symphony to your Souls..."
Anonymous